WHY WE
KEEP CLEAN

by Rosalyn Clark

BUMBA BOOKS™

LERNER PUBLICATIONS ◆ MINNEAPOLIS

Note to Educators:

Throughout this book, you'll find critical thinking questions. These can be used to engage young readers in thinking critically about the topic and in using the text and photos to do so.

Lerner Publications Company
A division of Lerner Publishing Group, Inc.
241 First Avenue North
Minneapolis, MN 55401 USA

For reading levels and more information, look up this title at www.lernerbooks.com.

Library of Congress Cataloging-in-Publication Data

The Cataloging-in-Publication Data for *Why We Keep Clean* is on file at the Library of Congress.
ISBN 978-1-5124-8294-2 (lib. bdg.)
ISBN 978-1-5415-1111-8 (pbk.)
ISBN 978-1-5124-8301-7 (EB pdf)

Manufactured in the United States of America
1 – CG – 12/31/17

Expand learning beyond the printed book. Download free, complementary educational resources for this book from our website, www.lerneresource.com.

Table of Contents

Keeping Clean

We bathe.

We scrub.

There are many ways we keep clean.

Germs get on our skin.

Some germs can make

us sick.

We wash our hands before eating.

We wash our hands after using the bathroom.

This helps get rid of bad germs.

Can you think of other times when you should wash your hands?

Dirt gets on our skin.

Soap removes dirt.

We wash between our fingers. We wash around our fingernails. Germs can hide in these places.

How do you think germs get between our fingers?

13

It is time for a bath!

We clean our skin with soap.

We use shampoo to clean our hair.

Next we floss and brush our teeth.

We use toothpaste.

Toothpaste keeps our mouths clean.

Do you know how often you should floss and brush your teeth?

We change into

clean pajamas.

It is time for bed!

Everybody gets dirty.

How do you keep clean?

Washing Your Hands

1 Wet your hands.

2 Add soap and lather.

3 Be sure to scrub the backs of your hands.

4 Don't forget to wash in between your fingers!

5 Rinse the soap away with water.

6 Dry your hands.

Picture Glossary

dirt

something such as mud or dust that makes things unclean

germs

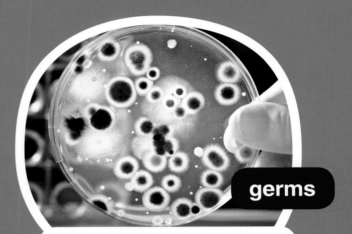

tiny living things that can cause disease and make us sick

scrub

to clean something by rubbing

shampoo

a liquid soap used for washing hair

Read More

Bellisario, Gina. *Take a Bath! My Tips for Keeping Clean.* Minneapolis: Millbrook Press, 2014.

Cleland, Joann. *Clean Hands, Dirty Hands.* Vero Beach, FL: Rourke Educational Media, 2013.

Hewitt, Sally. *Keeping Healthy.* Irvine, CA: Quarto Library, 2015.

Index

Photo Credits